Envision It! | Visual Skills Handbook

Cause and Effect

Draw Conclusions

Facts and Details

Literary Elements

Cause and Effect

Cause

Effect

Draw Conclusions

= Sad

Facts and Details

Literary Elements

Characters

BROTHER

MOMMY

DADDY

SISTER

Setting

Plot

Beginning

Middle

Theme

End

Envision It! | Visual Strategies Handbook

Background Knowledge

Important Ideas

Inferring

Monitor and Clarify

Predict and Set Purpose

Questioning

Story Structure

Summarize

Text Structure

Visualize

Background Knowledge

Let's Think About Reading!

- What do I already know?
- What does this remind me of?

Important Ideas

Inferring

Let's Think About Reading!

- What do I already know?
- How does this help me understand what happened?

Monitor and Clarify

Let's Think About Reading!

- What does not make sense?
- How can I fix it?

Predict and Set Purpose

Let's Think About Reading!

- What do I already know?
- What do I think will happen?
- What is my purpose for reading?

Questioning

Let's **Think** About **Reading!**

- What questions do I have about what I am reading?

Story Structure

Beginning

Middle

End

Let's Think About Reading!

- What happens in the beginning?
- What happens in the middle?
- What happens in the end?

Summarize

The dog knocked over the table.

Let's Think About Reading!

- What happens in the story?
- What is the story mainly about?

Text Structure

Let's Think About Reading!

- How is the story organized?
- Are there any patterns?

Visualize

Let's **Think** About **Reading!**

- What pictures do I see in my mind?

Program Authors

Peter Afflerbach

Camille Blachowicz

Candy Dawson Boyd

Elena Izquierdo

Connie Juel

Edward Kame'enui

Donald Leu

Jeanne R. Paratore

P. David Pearson

Sam Sebesta

Deborah Simmons

Alfred Tatum

Sharon Vaughn

Susan Watts Taffe

Karen Kring Wixson

Glenview, Illinois • Boston, Massachusetts • Chandler, Arizona •
Upper Saddle River, New Jersey

We dedicate Reading Street to
Peter Jovanovich.

His wisdom, courage,
and passion for education
are an inspiration to us all.

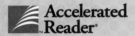

About the Cover Artist
Daniel Moreton lives in New York City, where he uses his computer to create illustrations for books. He has two dogs—basset hounds named Zoey and Eddie.

ISBN-13: 978-0-328-45558-4
ISBN-10:   0-328-45558-X
7 8 9 10 V042 14 13 12
CC1

Dear Reader,

What interesting things have you learned in your travels down *Scott Foresman Reading Street?* What interesting people have you met along the way?

In this book you will read about treasures. What things do you treasure? We hope you will treasure the stories and articles that we have included in this book. They are about surprising treasures and treasures we share!

Have fun exploring the interesting information you will find on *Scott Foresman Reading Street!*

Sincerely,
The Authors

Treasures

What do we treasure?

Week 2

Week 3

Unit 4 Contents

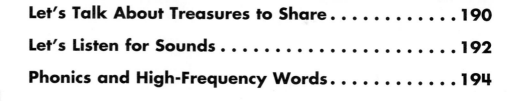
Week 6

Envision It! A Comprehension Handbook

Don Leu
The Internet Guy

Right before our eyes, the nature of reading and learning is changing. The Internet and other technologies create new opportunities, new solutions, and new literacies. New reading comprehension skills are required online. They are increasingly important to our students and our society.

Those of us on the Reading Street team are here to help you on this new, and very exciting, journey.

See It!

- **Big Question Video**

- **Concept Talk Video**

- **Envision It! Animations**

- **eReaders**

- **Interactive Sound-Spelling Cards**

bread

ea

Hear It!

- *Sing with Me* **Animations**

- **eSelections**

- **Grammar Jammer**

pronouns

I, me, he, she, they, we

- **Vocabulary Activities**

Concept Talk Video

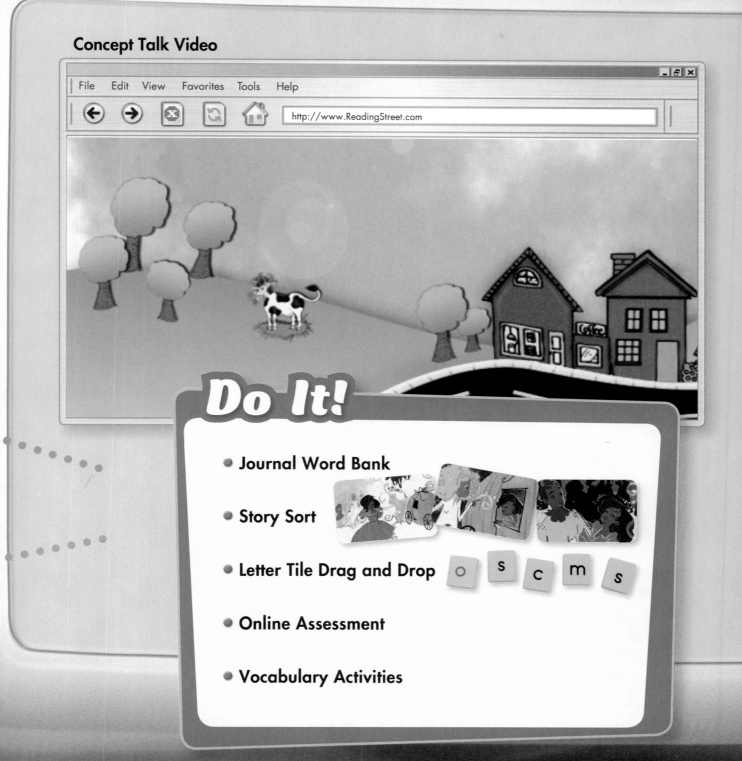

File   Edit   View   Favorites   Tools   Help

http://www.ReadingStreet.com

Do It!

- **Journal Word Bank**

- **Story Sort**

- **Letter Tile Drag and Drop**

- **Online Assessment**

- **Vocabulary Activities**

Treasures

What do we treasure?

Objectives
● Listen closely to speakers and ask questions to help you better understand the topic. ● Share information and ideas about the topic. Speak at the correct pace.

Oral Vocabulary

Read Together

Let's Talk About

Surprising Treasures

● Share ideas about what it means to treasure something.

● Share ideas about surprises.

● Take part in a discussion about how a surprise can be a treasure.

READING STREET ONLINE
CONCEPT TALK VIDEO
www.ReadingStreet.com

so far this year!

Let's Listen for

Sounds

● Find five things that contain the long *a* sound.

● Find three things that rhyme with *main*. Say the last sound in those words.

● Find a picture of a chain. Now change the sound /ch/ in *chain* to /r/. Say the new word.

● Find something that rhymes with *pail*. Now say each sound in that word.

READING STREET ONLINE
SOUND-SPELLING CARDS
www.ReadingStreet.com

Read Together

14

15

Envision It! | Sounds to Know

snail

ai

hay

ay

READING STREET ONLINE
SOUND-SPELLING CARDS
www.ReadingStreet.com

Phonics

Vowel Digraphs *ai, ay*

Words I Can Blend

p	ai	d
t	r	ai	n
g	r	ay
s	t	ay
t	ai	l

Sentences I Can Read

1. She paid for a ride on this train.

2. We like to stay in on a gray morning.

3. My cat has a long tail.

High-Frequency Words

Words I Can Read

give

surprise

would

enjoy

worry

about

Sentences I Can Read

1. Mom may give Liz a surprise party.
2. Would Ray enjoy painting?
3. Dad stays close when we worry about stuff.

Envision It! | **Sounds to Know**

dog's bone

singular possessive

boys' bedroom

plural possessive

Phonics

🔁 Singular and Plural Possessives

Words I Can Blend

R o b 's   h a t

p i g s'   p e n

C a m 's   b a g

T e s s 's   b e d

k i d s'   d o g

Sentences I Can Read

1. Rob's hat fell in the pigs' pen.

2. Is Cam's bag on Tess's bed?

3. The kids' dog is big and soft.

Last May, Kait and Fay rode the train on Main Street to give their moms a surprise. Those moms would enjoy shopping!

Kait's mom got on at that train's first stop. Fay's mom got on at its third stop, Bay Street. The girls' moms nodded hi and waited for Kait and Fay to sit with them.

Then it started raining. Did those girls worry about it? No, but that rain was a pain!

You've learned

- Vowel Digraphs *ai, ay*
- Singular and Plural Possessives

High-Frequency Words

give surprise would

enjoy worry about

Mama's Birthday Present

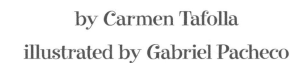

by Carmen Tafolla

illustrated by Gabriel Pacheco

Genre

Realistic fiction is a made-up story that could really happen. Next you will read about a birthday surprise. What do you want to find out? Set a purpose for reading.

Read Together

20

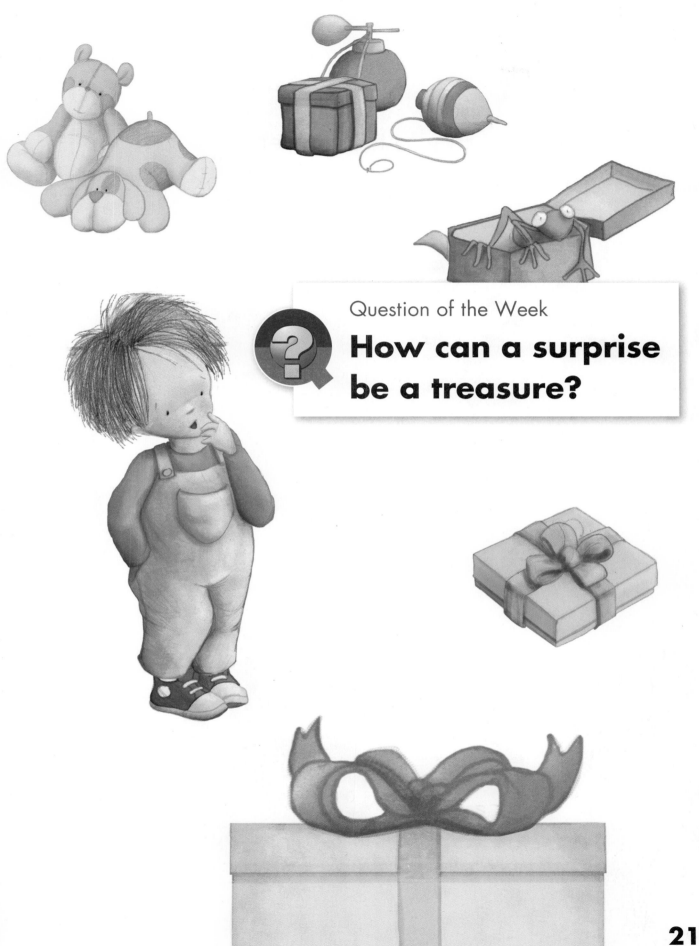

Question of the Week

How can a surprise be a treasure?

Francisco ran into the garden.
His grandmother was reading a book.

"Grandma! Grandma!" called Francisco.
"Next Sunday is Mama's birthday! Mama
always surprises me with a party for my
birthday. Can we surprise Mama with a party?"

"That is a wonderful idea, Francisco," said Grandma. "Today is Monday. If we begin today, we will have seven days to plan a party."

"Mama always gives me a present for my birthday," said Francisco. "What present can I give Mama?"

"I don't know," said Grandma. "But don't worry. We can make a piñata to break. Your mama will enjoy that."

So Grandma and Francisco made a piñata.

On Tuesday, Francisco wondered about
Mama's present. Francisco went to talk with
Papa about Mama's birthday party.

"What present can I give Mama?"
asked Francisco.

"I don't know," said Papa. "But don't worry. I can play my guitar. Your mama will enjoy that."

So Papa promised Francisco he would play his guitar.

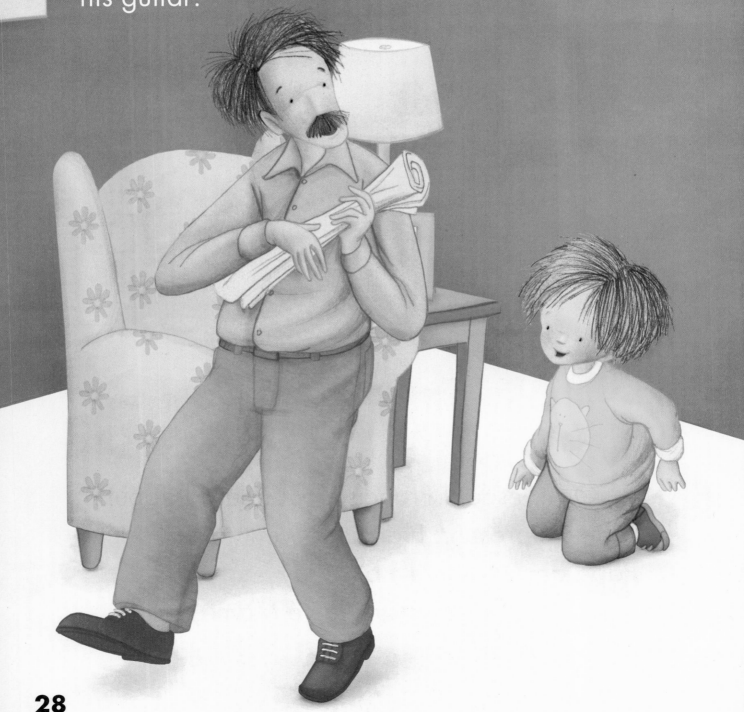

On Wednesday, Francisco wondered about Mama's present. Francisco and his older brother went to invite Señora Molina to Mama's party. Señora Molina had a tortilla shop.

"What present can I give Mama?"
asked Francisco.

"I don't know," said Señora Molina. "But
don't worry. I can bring some hot tortillas,
fresh off the stove. Your mama will enjoy that."

So Señora Molina promised Francisco she
would bring hot tortillas, fresh off the stove.

On Thursday, Francisco wondered about Mama's present. He went to talk to his friend Gina about it.

"What present can I give Mama?" asked Francisco.

"I don't know," said Gina. "But don't worry. We can make confetti eggs to crack on people's heads. Your mama will enjoy that."

So Gina and Francisco filled and painted the bright confetti eggs.

On Friday, Francisco wondered about
Mama's present. So he went to speak to
Grandpa Pérez.

"What present can I give Mama?"
asked Francisco.

"I don't know," said Grandpa Pérez. "But don't worry. We can make some sweet buñuelos. Your mama will enjoy that."

So Francisco and Grandpa Pérez made some sweet buñuelos.

On Saturday, Francisco still wondered about his present for Mama. But Francisco had many things to do.

He helped his brothers
and sisters look for a place
to hang the piñata.

He talked to Papa
about the songs Papa
would play on his guitar.

He talked to Señora Molina
about the tortillas she would bring.

He found a
safe place to hide
Gina's confetti eggs

and Grandpa Pérez's
sweet buñuelos.

Everyone was ready for Mama's surprise.

On Sunday, everyone came to the party. Mama was very surprised.

Papa played his guitar. Señora Molina's hot tortillas smelled wonderful. Grandpa's sweet buñuelos tasted wonderful.

Everyone ate and sang and had fun. The children cracked confetti eggs over everyone's heads. Then they all lined up to take a swing at the piñata.

Everyone looked happy. Everyone
except Francisco.
    "Francisco, what is the matter?"
asked Mama.
    "I did not know what to give you for your
birthday, Mama."

"Oh, Francisco," said Mama. "This party was the best present you could give me. No, the second best."

"Second best?" asked Francisco.

41

"Yes. The best present of all is having my family and friends here with me. That is the most wonderful part of a party!"

Mama gave Francisco a big hug. Then they all took turns hitting the piñata. The one who broke it was Francisco.

And Mama enjoyed that.

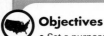

Envision It! | Retell

**READING STREET ONLINE
STORY SORT**
www.ReadingStreet.com

44

Think Critically

1. What advice would you have given Francisco about what to give Mama? **Text to Self**

2. How does the author show how Francisco's family cares about one another?

Think Like an Author

3. Why was a gift for Mama so important to Francisco?

Draw Conclusions

4. Look back at page 30. Read the words. If you didn't know what the word *tortillas* meant, try reading the words again if you still don't understand.

Monitor and Clarify

5. Look Back and Write
Look back at pages 40–43. What is Mama's birthday present from Francisco? Write about it.

TEST PRACTICE Extended Response

Meet the Author

Carmen Tafolla

Carmen Tafolla grew up in San Antonio, Texas. She tells stories and writes poems about her Mexican American neighborhood.

Dr. Tafolla works with schools around the world to help children of all races and languages to succeed. She lives in a hundred-year-old house in San Antonio with her husband, son, mother, and lots of books.

Here are more books about treasures.

Use the Reading Log in the *Reader's and Writer's Notebook* to record your independent reading.

Objectives
● Write short letters that put your ideas in an order that makes sense and uses the correct features.
● Understand and use adjectives when reading, writing, and speaking.

Descriptive

Key Features of a Friendly Letter

● written to someone the writer knows

● has a polite greeting and closing

READING STREET ONLINE
GRAMMAR JAMMER
www.ReadingStreet.com

Friendly Letter

A **friendly letter** can tell someone about your ideas or feelings. The student model on the next page is an example of a friendly letter.

Writing Prompt Think about a surprise you would like to give as a gift. Now write a letter telling a friend or family member about your idea.

Writer's Checklist

Remember, you should . . .

☑ write a letter to a friend or someone in your family.

☑ write your ideas in an order that makes sense.

☑ use adjectives to describe the surprise.

Dear Mom,

   I plan to surprise Dad on his birthday. We can bring him breakfast in bed. First, we can serve yummy eggs. Next, we can give him big pancakes. They are his favorite foods.

            Your son,
            Matt

Genre Friendly Letter The writer tells ideas to someone he knows, his mom.

Writing Trait Organization The sentences are in an order that makes sense.

These **adjectives** tell about food.

Conventions

Adjectives

Remember An **adjective** tells more about a person, place, animal, or thing.

A **tall** man pats the **cute** puppy.

I saw a **red** rug at the **new** store.

47

Social Studies in Reading

Genre
Recipe

Read Together

● A recipe is procedural text. It is a set of directions that tells how to make something to eat or drink.

● It is important to follow a recipe in the order in which it is written.

● A recipe may have pictures and numbers. Both help us understand what to do first, next, and last.

● As you read "Limonada Recipe," look for elements that make it a recipe.

Limonada
Recipe

Limonada means "lemonade" in Spanish. Here is a recipe for this cool drink. Serve it at your next party!

What You Need

large pitcher

8 lemons, cut in half

1 gallon of cold water

2 cups of sugar

What You Do

1. Squeeze the juice from the lemon halves into the pitcher.

2. Add the water to the lemon juice and stir.

3. Add the sugar to the lemon juice and water, and stir.

4. Pour the limonada into cups and serve.

Let's **Think** About...

What are the steps in making *limonada*? **Recipe**

Let's **Think** About...

Where could you look if you had trouble understanding the things you need to make lemonade? **Recipe**

Let's **Think** About...

Reading Across Texts Why would *limonada* be a good thing to have at the party in *Mama's Birthday Present*?

Writing Across Texts In *Mama's Birthday Present*, Francisco plans a birthday party for his mother. Write his plan as a set of directions with pictures.

Let's Learn It!

Read Together

READING STREET ONLINE
VOCABULARY ACTIVITIES
www.ReadingStreet.com

Get Ready For Grade 2

Use descriptive words so that others can "see" what you're talking about.

Listening and Speaking

Give Descriptions When we give descriptions, we use words to tell how things look, sound, and feel. We stay on topic, speaking clearly so that people can understand us. Descriptive adjectives help others "see" what we are talking about.

Practice It! Imagine that you are at a birthday party. Describe the party to others. Use descriptive adjectives to tell how things look, sound, and feel.

50

Vocabulary

Time and order words are words that tell us when events happen.

I will write the letter **before** bedtime.

I will go outside **after** lunch.

Before and **after** are examples of words that tell when we will do something.

Practice It! Draw three pictures of something that happens *before, during,* and *after.* Label each picture with the correct time and order word.

Fluency

Expression and Intonation When you read, try to read the sentences as if you are talking. Use your voice to express feeling.

Practice It!

1. Would Nell's train be late?

2. Jack's birthday card was a big surprise!

3. My sister's friend did not worry about the party.

Objectives
● Listen closely to speakers and ask questions to help you better understand the topic. ● Share information and ideas about the topic. Speak at the correct pace.

Read Together

Let's Talk About

Surprising Treasures

● Share ideas about what it means to treasure something.

● Discuss special stories we've heard over and over again.

● Discuss how a story can be a treasure.

READING STREET ONLINE
CONCEPT TALK VIDEO
www.ReadingStreet.com

THE
RIO
GRANDE

Objectives
- Know how a word changes when one of its sounds is changed.
- Combine sounds together to say words with one and two syllables.
- Pick out sounds at the beginning, in the middle, and at the end of one-syllable words.

Let's Listen for

Read Together

Sounds

- Find a picture of a bunny. Change the sound /b/ in *bunny* to the sound /s/. Say the new word.

- Find two things that rhyme with *reach*. Say the sound at the end of those words.

- Find something that rhymes with *head*. Say the sound in the middle of that word.

- Find three things that end in the long *e* sound.

**READING STREET ONLINE
SOUND-SPELLING CARDS**
www.ReadingStreet.com

54

1 + 5 = 6
5 + 2 = 7
3 + 5 = 8

55

Envision It! | Sounds to Know

easel

ea

bread

ea

READING STREET ONLINE
SOUND-SPELLING CARDS
www.ReadingStreet.com

Phonics

Vowel Digraph *ea*

Words I Can Blend

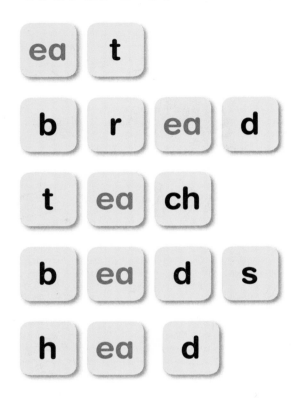

ea t

b r ea d

t ea ch

b ea d s

h ea d

Sentences I Can Read

1. We eat bread with lunch.

2. Can she teach me to string beads?

3. Ned put that silly hat on his head.

Words I Can Read

draw

colors

over

drew

great

sign

show

Sentences I Can Read

1. We can teach him to draw with five colors.

2. She drew six birds flying over that beach.

3. Dad read my sign about that great show.

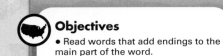

Objectives
● Read words that add endings to the main part of the word.

Phonics

Adding Endings

Words I Can Blend

h o b b ie s

c r ie d

e m p t ie d

t r ie s

p u p p ie s

Sentences I Can Read

1. Hobbies fill my time with fun.

2. Jill cried when Jack emptied his bucket.

3. Tom tries training his puppies to sit.

Sunday we will put on this great show. Jean will draw a sign and hang it up over her gate. Neal drew a stage set with many colors.

This show will star my puppies and Jean's bunnies. Jean has tried teaching her bunnies to hop.

My puppies bumped heads when they tried to play dead. This will be fun!

You've learned

◉ Vowel Digraph *ea*
◉ Adding Endings

High-Frequency Words
draw   colors   over   drew
great   sign   show

Cinderella

written by Teresa R. Roberts

illustrated by Paule Trudel

A **fairy tale** is a story whose characters can include princes and princesses. In this story you will read about a girl who wants to go to the prince's ball.

How can a story be a treasure?

Once upon a time, in a far-off land, over hills and past farms, lived a girl named Cinderella. Cindy, as she was called, was sweet and nice.

Cindy had two sisters. Roz and Gert were not so sweet or nice. They were mean. They made Cindy sweep, mop, scrub, and dust all day.

Each year the prince had a great ball at his castle. One day, a man came with a note. The prince asked the sisters to his ball.

"Maybe he will make me his wife!" Gert clapped her hands.

"No, he will not! It will be me!" Roz yelled.

"May I go as well?" asked Cindy.

"No!" cried her sisters.

"That rug needs beating!"

"This dish is filthy!"

"Stay home and clean, Cinderella!"

Cindy watched Roz and Gert try on dresses. Red! Green! White! Pink! Such nice colors! And the finest fabric stitched with the finest thread! All Cindy got was a dirty mop.

Cindy watched her sisters drive off.

She tried sweeping.
She tried dusting.
But she felt so sad.
She hung her head
and cried.

Rap, tap, tap. Rap, tap, tap.
A wise old woman came in.

She patted Cindy's hand. "I will help you go to the ball."

"But I cannot go in these rags!" Cindy wailed.

"Just wait and see. I will show you."

Snap! Cindy had a nice dress and glass slippers!

Snap! Snap! Six mice turned into horses!

Snap! Snap! Snap! That pumpkin turned into a flashy coach!

71

"It is time to go! But be back by twelve o'clock. The chimes will ring. That will be the sign that everything will turn back."

Cinderella went to the ball. She met the prince. They twirled and whirled in each other's arms all night.

Then the chimes started clanging. Cindy gasped and ran fast.

"Wait!" called the prince. "Stop!"

He did not see where Cindy went. She had lost her glass slipper on the top step.

Back at home, Cindy's sisters made her scrub, sweep, and mop. She no longer wore her fine dress. Cindy used her finger to draw a sad face in the dust at her feet. After she drew it, her tears fell into the dust.

Rap, tap, tap. It was the prince!

"Is this your glass slipper?" he asked Roz.

She tried it. It did not fit. Then Gert tried it. It did not fit.

76

But it *did* fit Cinderella. She and the prince married, and they lived happily ever after.

Envision It! Retell

Think Critically

1. What parts of this fairy tale remind you of other fairy tales you have heard or read? Text to Text

2. Why do you think the author wrote a new version of an old fairy tale?

Author's Purpose

3. What is the big idea of this fairy tale? Theme

4. Describe Cinderella and the ball at the castle as you see them in your mind. Visualize

5. Look Back and Write
Look back at page 68. Why is Cinderella sad? Write about it.

TEST PRACTICE Extended Response

Meet the Illustrator

Paule Trudel

Paule Trudel grew up in a house full of games, secret letters, and bedtime stories. When she was a little girl, she liked to dress up in costumes and pretend she was a princess. Her favorite fairy tale is *Snow White*.

Like Cinderella, Ms. Trudel had a wise old woman in her life: her Grandmother Helene, who taught her how to knit. Now, along with painting and drawing, knitting is one of Ms. Trudel's favorite pastimes.

Here are other books that tell the story of Cinderella.

Reading Log

Use the Reading Log in the *Reader's and Writer's Notebook* to record your independent reading.

79

Objectives

● Write short letters that put your ideas in an order that makes sense and uses the correct features.

● Understand and use adjectives when reading, writing, and speaking.

Let's Write It!

Read Together

Key Features of an Invitation

● asks people to come to an event

● tells important information about the event

READING STREET ONLINE
GRAMMAR JAMMER
www.ReadingStreet.com

Invitation

An **invitation** asks a person to come to an event and tells about the event. The student model on the next page is an example of an invitation.

Writing Prompt Think of how people plan events, such as a party or family dinner. Write an invitation to an event.

Writer's Checklist

Remember, you should . . .

☑ ask someone to an event using polite words.

☑ write the date correctly.

☑ tell the event's date, time, and place.

☑ write your ideas in an order that makes sense.

☑ use adjectives that describe.

80

March 1, 2010

Dear Leon,

Please come to my birthday party. It will be on Saturday, March 15, at 1:00 p.m.

My house is on Elm Street. Look for the green balloons!

Your friend,

Maria

Genre
The **invitation** includes the date and tells when and where the party will be.

Writing Trait Word Choice
The writer uses the polite word *Please.*

This **adjective** names a color.

Conventions

- **Adjectives (Colors and Shapes)**

  Some **adjectives** tell colors. Some adjectives tell shapes.

- She draws a **square** box with a **blue** flower in it.

Social Studies in Reading

Anarosa

written by Luc Sanchez
illustrated by Luciana Navarro Powell

Genre
Fairy Tale

- A fairy tale is a story whose characters often include kings, queens, princes, or princesses. These characters must solve a problem.

- A fairy tale often begins with the phrase "Once upon a time." This phrase tells readers that the story has been told for a long time, and that it is make-believe.

- A fairy tale often ends with the phrase "and they lived happily ever after." This phrase means everything turns out well for the characters.

- As you read "Anarosa," think about what makes it a fairy tale.

Once upon a time, Anarosa lived with Tía Lola and her cousins, Esmeralda and Rima. Tía Lola made Anarosa scrub and sweep all day. Anarosa worked hard and did not complain.

82

Esmeralda and Rima were going to the grand fiesta. Anarosa watched. She wanted to go too. But Tía Lola told her she must stay home and work.

Let's **Think** About...

With what phrase does the story begin? What does this tell you about the story?
Fairy Tale

Let's **Think** About...

What is Anarosa's problem?
Fairy Tale

Let's Think About...

What does Anarosa do about her problem?
Fairy Tale

Anarosa swept the floors quickly and made them sparkle. She grabbed a bow for her hair. She found a beautiful dress. Then she hurried off to the fiesta.

Anarosa ran right into the prince! He thought she was charming. They danced all night. Anarosa became Princess Anarosa, and they lived happily ever after.

Let's Think About...

With what phrase does the story end? What does this mean for Anarosa and the prince? **Fairy Tale**

Let's Think About...

Reading Across Texts How are Cinderella and Anarosa alike? How are they different?

Writing Across Texts If Cinderella and Anarosa met, what do you think they would say to each other? Write about it.

Let's Learn It!

Read Together

READING STREET ONLINE
VOCABULARY ACTIVITIES
www.ReadingStreet.com

I think we should choose this book because it is a good story. The characters are funny. Which book would you like us to choose, Maria?

Get Ready For Grade 2

In group discussions, respond when someone calls your name.

Listening and Speaking

Share Information and Ideas A good listener pays attention to what others say and listens carefully to different ideas. Let everyone have a chance to speak.

Practice It! Work with some of your classmates to choose a new book. Give everyone a chance to share ideas.

Vocabulary

A **compound word** is a word made up of two smaller words. You can find the meaning of the word by looking at the two smaller words.

mailbox = mail + box

Mail is letters and packages. A *box* is a place to put things. A *mailbox* is a box where you put mail.

Practice It! Read these compound words. Say the meaning of each word.

bathtub   sandbox   handshake

Fluency

Accuracy and Rate Read the sentences. Read at a pace so you understand the text. Blend the sounds to read new words. Check the new words in the sentence to be sure they make sense.

Practice It!

1. Neal has a sandbox in his backyard.

2. Gabby tried to draw a leaf.

3. Lea hurried over to the beach.

Oral Vocabulary

Read Together

Let's Talk About

Surprising Treasures

● Share ideas about what it means to treasure something.

● Share information about treasures we can find in our country.

READING STREET ONLINE
CONCEPT TALK VIDEO
www.ReadingStreet.com

You've learned
2 0 5
Amazing Words
so far this year!

89

Objectives
• Know how a word changes when one of its sounds is changed.
• Combine sounds together to say words with one and two syllables.
• Break up one-syllable words into each sound that makes up the word.

Let's Listen for

Read Together

Sounds

● Find five things that contain the long *o* sound.

● Look at the flag blow in the wind. Change the sounds /bl/ in *blow* to /gl/. Say the new word.

● Find something that rhymes with *flat*. Now slowly say each sound in that word.

● Find something that begins with the sounds /spr/. Say each sound in that word.

READING STREET ONLINE
SOUND-SPELLING CARDS
www.ReadingStreet.com

BAIT SHOP

90

Envision It! | Sounds to Know

soap

oa

snow

ow

READING STREET ONLINE
SOUND-SPELLING CARDS
www.ReadingStreet.com

Phonics

🎯 Vowel Digraphs *oa, ow*

Words I Can Blend

s   n   ow

r   oa   d

s   oa   k   s

b   ow   l

f   l   oa   t

Sentences I Can Read

1. Snow piles up on this road.

2. Mom soaks beans in a bowl.

3. He can float his raft on Long Lake.

Words I Can Read

once

found

wild

took

mouth

Sentences I Can Read

1. We once found five toads under this big tree.

2. Show me that wild crow.

3. Joan took her toast and put it in her mouth.

Envision It! | **Sounds to Know**

splash

3-letter blend

READING STREET ONLINE
SOUND-SPELLING CARDS
www.ReadingStreet.com

Phonics

🕐 Three-Letter Consonant Blends

Words I Can Blend

s t r o ng

s p r ea d

th r oa t

sh r u b s

s p r i ng

Sentences I Can Read

1. We drank strong tea and spread butter on bread.

2. My throat feels sore.

3. Shrubs turn green in spring.

Once last spring, we found a wild toad squatting under the low branch of an oak tree. It had stripes on its back, a pale throat, and strong back legs. A funny croak came from its wide mouth.

We were thrilled! We picked up the toad to show Mom. When Mom spotted the toad, she screamed, "Scram, toad!"

"Let's split," I said, and we took the toad back to the oak tree.

You've learned

- Vowel Digraphs *oa, ow*
- Three-Letter Consonant Blends

High-Frequency Words
once   found   wild
took   mouth

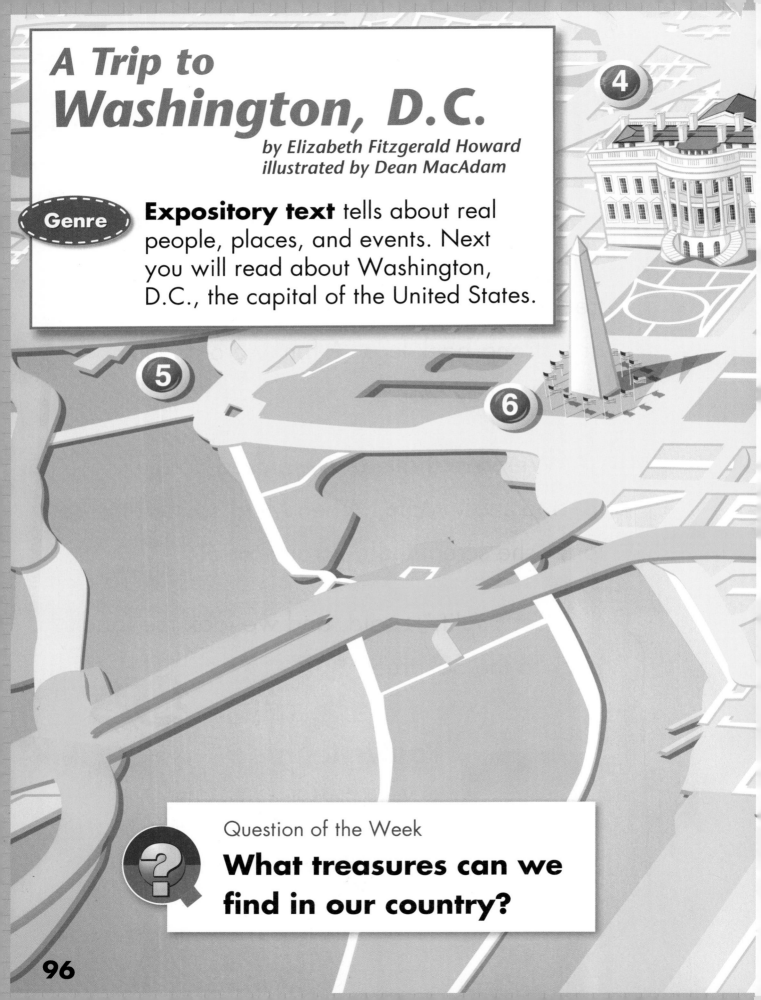

A Trip to
Washington, D.C.

by Elizabeth Fitzgerald Howard
illustrated by Dean MacAdam

Genre

Expository text tells about real people, places, and events. Next you will read about Washington, D.C., the capital of the United States.

Question of the Week

What treasures can we find in our country?

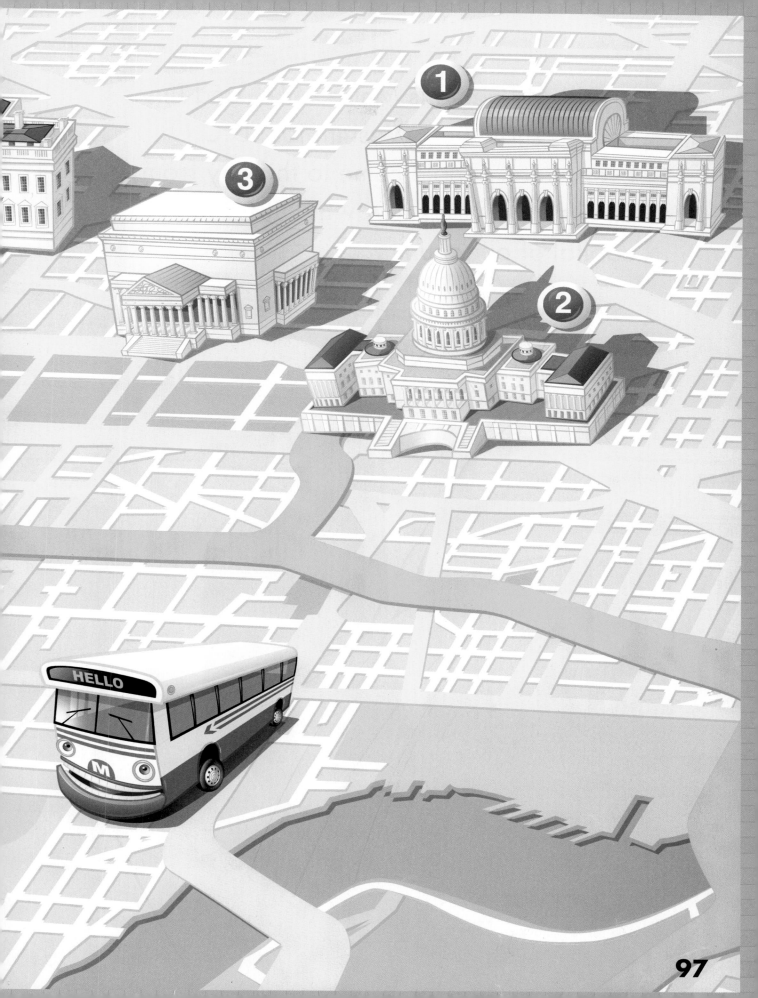

Hi! My name is Metro Mike, and I'm here to show you Washington, D.C.! Every year people come to this city from all over. Do you know why? It is the capital of our country.

Come with me! I'll show you this splendid city. Sometimes I have a busload of people. But now this coach is just for you.

In Washington, D.C., the leaders of our country make laws. Laws are rules we follow. How do those people become our leaders? We vote for them. When people vote, they pick who will make the laws that we all follow.

Our first stop is on your left. That's the home of two documents. One is the Declaration of Independence. That paper says that Americans have the right to be free. The other is the U.S. Constitution. It is the plan for our government.

Declaration of Independence

Constitution

Washington, D.C., was named after George Washington, our first President. The President is the leader of our country. Many people call George Washington the "Father of Our Country."

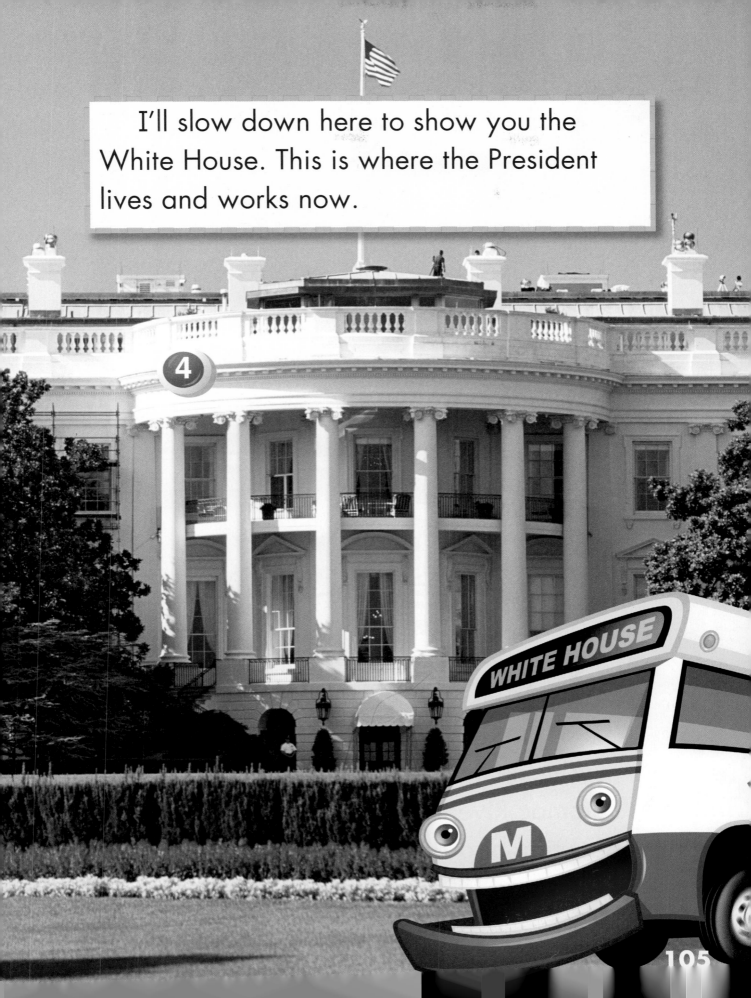

I'll slow down here to show you the White House. This is where the President lives and works now.

WHITE HOUSE

This next road will take us by the Potomac River. Look up in the sky! That beautiful bird stands for America. It is strong and free!

Did you see that splash? That bird took a fish to put in its mouth. Once there weren't many of these birds in the wild. Now there are many more.

Down that street you'll see lots of flags! In Washington, D.C., you will see the Stars and Stripes flying in many places. This red, white, and blue flag also stands for America.

6

We are back at the start. I hope you found Washington, D.C., to be a great city. Come back again soon!

Objectives
- Read on your own for a period of time. • Tell the main idea of an article that you heard or read.
- Write short comments on stories, poems, and nonfiction articles that have information.

Envision It! | Retell

Think Critically

 Read Together

1. Why is the capital of our country an important place? Text to World

2. Why does the author write about buildings in our capital? Author's Purpose

3. Whom was our capital named after? Why?

   Facts and Details

4. Name two things that stand for America. Important Ideas

5. **Look Back and Write** Look back at the selection. Write about one thing you can see in Washington, D.C.

   TEST PRACTICE Extended Response

Elizabeth Fitzgerald Howard

When she is not writing about important places such as Washington, D.C., Elizabeth Fitzgerald Howard often writes stories based on people in her family. Her father told her many stories about his family and childhood while she was growing up. After she retired from teaching, Ms. Howard turned several family stories into children's books.

Here are more books by Elizabeth Fitzgerald Howard.

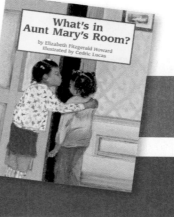

 Use the Reading Log in the *Reader's and Writer's Notebook* to record your independent reading.

111

Objectives
● Write short poems that have details one can see, smell, hear, taste, or touch. ● Understand and use adjectives when reading, writing, and speaking.

Descriptive

Read Together

Key Features of a Descriptive Poem

● most are shorter than a story

● words describe and can rhyme or not rhyme

**READING STREET ONLINE
GRAMMAR JAMMER**
www.ReadingStreet.com

Descriptive Poem

A **descriptive poem** helps readers make a picture in their minds. The student model on the next page is an example of a descriptive poem.

Writing Prompt Think about a field trip you would like to take. Write a poem describing what you would like to see.

Writer's Checklist

Remember, you should . . .

☑ help readers make a picture in their minds.

☑ focus on one place you would like to see.

☑ use adjectives to describe things, including their size.

The Best Field Trip

Let's take a trip to a big zoo!
We will see huge bears
and a tall kangaroo!
We can see a tiny mouse
in a little house.

Writing Trait Focus/Ideas This poem **focuses** on one main place.

These **adjectives** tell about size.

Genre Descriptive Poem This poem describes animals and a zoo.

Conventions

- ## Adjectives for Size

  Remember Some **adjectives** tell about size. **Big, small, long**, and **short** describe size.

  That is a **big** flag.

113

Genre
Autobiography

Read Together

- An autobiography is the story of someone's life told by that person.

- The author of an autobiography uses the words *I* and *me* when talking about his or her life.

- An autobiography is about real people and places. The events that take place are true.

- As you read "My 4th of July," think about what makes it an autobiography.

My 4th of July

My family has fun on the 4th of July. Mom bakes eight pies to share at the block party.

Let's Think About...

What part of the author's life is the author describing? **Autobiography**

We wrap red, white, and blue ribbons on our bikes.

We laugh as we try to win the sack race.

Let's **Think** About...

What **sensory details** can you find? How do they help you see and hear what the writer describes?
Autobiography

Let's **Think** About...

How can you tell that this selection is an autobiography?
Autobiography

Dad knows the best place to watch the fireworks at night. Crack! Bang! They light up the sky above us.

116

Will the fireworks touch the moon? We laugh and cheer. What a beautiful sight!

Let's **Think** About...

Is this selection a true story or a fantasy? Explain why. **Autobiography**

Let's **Think** About...

Reading Across Texts *A Trip to Washington, D.C.* and "My 4th of July" tell about things that are important to Americans. Describe these things.

Writing Across Texts If the author of "My 4th of July" visited Washington, D.C., with relatives, what might they do there? Write about it.

Let's
Learn
It!

Read
Together

READING STREET ONLINE
VOCABULARY ACTIVITIES
www.ReadingStreet.com

Listening and Speaking

Get Ready For
Grade 2

Use your voice to show a poem's rhythm.

Poetry Presentation When we read a poem, we use our voices to show the rhythm of the poem. A rhythm is a strong beat. We speak clearly so others can understand.

 Write a short poem about Washington, D.C. Read it to others. Use your voice to show the rhythm.

Vocabulary

Words can be sorted into groups. **Nouns** are words that name people, animals, places, or things. **Verbs** are words that name actions.

boat

run

Boat is a noun. *Run* is a verb.

Practice It! Read these words. Sort and write the words into groups of nouns and verbs.

tree   **jump**   **cry**   **bird**

Fluency

Expression and Intonation When you read, try to read the sentences as if you are talking. Use your voice to show feeling.

Practice It!

1. We painted wild stripes on our boat.

2. Kate saw a crow as we rowed down the stream.

3. We found a toad that has a huge mouth!

Oral Vocabulary

Read Together

Let's Talk About

Treasures to Share

- Share ideas about what it means to share a treasure.

- Share ideas about why we treasure special places.

READING STREET ONLINE
CONCEPT TALK VIDEO
www.ReadingStreet.com

STATE FAIR TEXAS

SUPER MIDWAY

SUPER MIDWAY

Objectives
- Know how a word changes when one of its sounds is changed. ● Pick out sounds at the beginning, in the middle, and at the end of one-syllable words. ● Break up one-syllable words into each sound that makes up the word.

Phonemic Awareness

Let's Listen for

Sounds

- Find the delivery person wearing a tie. Change the sound /t/ in *tie* to the sound /p/. Say the new word.

- One of the boys is in a field. Say each sound in the word *field*.

- Grandma is eating a piece of pie. Say the sound at the beginning of *piece* and *pie*.

- Find something that rhymes with *tight*. Say each sound in that word.

READING STREET ONLINE
SOUND-SPELLING CARDS
www.ReadingStreet.com

Envision It! | **Sounds to Know**

field

ie

pie

ie

lightbulb

igh

Phonics

Vowel Digraphs *ie, igh*

Words I Can Blend

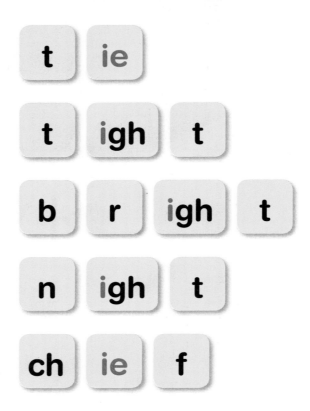

t ie

t igh t

b r igh t

n igh t

ch ie f

Sentences I Can Read

1. Please tie my laces tight.

2. Show me that bright star in the night sky.

3. The fire chief has a truck.

Words I Can Read

eight

moon

touch

above

laugh

Sentences I Can Read

1. For eight nights, that bright moon shone in the sky.

2. Mike can touch that light above his head.

3. We laugh when my puppy grabs his piece of meat.

knight

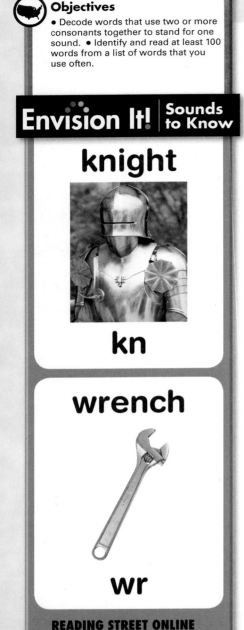

kn

wrench

wr

Phonics

Consonant Patterns *kn, wr*

Words I Can Blend

kn o ck

wr i t e

kn ow

wr a p

kn o t

Sentences I Can Read

1. Knock on that wall.

2. We know when to write.

3. Tom will wrap that gift and tie its ribbon in a big knot.

My niece Mandy wrote about the moon. For eight nights, she checked out that moon above Smiths' field.

Did you know the moon seems to change shape? It might be bright, or it might not show light. That moon might seem close enough to touch.

Some nights Mandy wants to tie a knot around that moon and bring it close. That would make her laugh!

You've learned

- Vowel Digraphs *ie, igh*
- Consonant Patterns *kn, wr*

High-Frequency Words

eight   moon   above

touch   laugh

A Southern Ranch

by Yossel Ayarzagoitia Riesenfeld

Genre

Expository text tells about real people, places, and events. In this selection you will read about a ranch in the southern part of the United States.

The sun isn't up yet, and high above the land, the moon still gleams in dark skies. But lights are on in this place. Another day is starting on the ranch.

Ranches are places that raise livestock. Horses, cows, sheep, and goats are livestock. This ranch raises cows, or cattle. Ranch hands help look after the livestock and the ranch.

Ranch hands no longer take cattle up long trails. Ranch hands may drive pickup trucks. But they are still much like ranch hands long ago.

Ranch hands still ride horses and use lassos. They still care for sick animals. Ranch hands still watch herds of cattle.

If cattle go the wrong way, ranch hands must lead them the right way. In summer, if herds eat all the grass in one place, ranch hands take them to another place. In winter, ranch hands feed herds hay and grain.

Roundups take place in spring and fall. Ranch hands go out in the field and look for cows. This is not an easy job. Cows might be standing under a tree or grazing at the bottom of a hill.

After getting eight or ten cows, ranch hands must keep them together and keep them walking. Cows might run off. Ranch hands must chase them and bring them back.

Ranch hands need well-trained horses for this work. These horses can be steered by just a touch, and they know cows!

Sometimes cattle dogs help keep the cows together too.

Ranch hands bring small bunches of cows to the same spot. Nine or ten become forty or fifty.

Then ranch hands bring those bigger bunches to another spot. In time, the herd might number 600 or more.

Keeping this big herd together is hard. Some ranch hands ride "point," or in front. Some ride "swing," or on each side. Some ride "drag," or in back. That is a dusty job!

Ranch hands take the herd to the ranch. Those cows that are being sold are loaded on trucks and shipped off. The rest will be sent back to graze on more grass.

Roundup has ended. After so much time on horseback, weary ranch hands can rest. They eat and talk and laugh. Then it's back to work on the ranch.

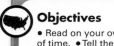

Envision It! | **Retell**

READING STREET ONLINE STORY SORT
www.ReadingStreet.com

144

Think Critically

1. What part of a ranch hand's job would you like most to do? Text to Self

2. Why does the author explain what ranches and cattle are? Think Like an Author

3. What helps ranch hands on roundups? Facts and Details

4. What questions did you ask yourself as you read the selection? Questioning

5. Look Back and Write
Look back at pages 136–137. How do ranch hands keep the herd together? Write about it.

TEST PRACTICE | Extended Response

Yossel Ayarzagoitia Riesenfeld

Yossel Ayarzagoitia Riesenfeld was born in Texas, but he grew up in Monterrey, Mexico. Once a soccer coach in the Chicago area, he now referees children's soccer games.

Mr. Ayarzagoitia Riesenfeld enjoys playing soccer, watching sports on television, teaching Spanish, and traveling. He has visited several ranches, and although he has never ridden a horse, he once rode a donkey at a picnic in Mexico!

Here are other books about ranches and ranch animals.

Use the Reading Log in the *Reader's and Writer's Notebook* to record your independent reading.

Let's Write It!

Read Together

Key Features of a Realistic Story

● has characters and a setting that seem real

● tells events that could really happen

● has a beginning, middle, and end

READING STREET ONLINE
GRAMMAR JAMMER
www.ReadingStreet.com

Realistic Story

A **realistic story** is a made-up story that could happen in real life. The student model on the next page is an example of a realistic story.

Writing Prompt Think about life on a ranch. Write a story about children who visit or live on a ranch.

Writer's Checklist

Remember, you should . . .

☑ tell story events that could really happen.

☑ include sentences that are not all alike.

☑ use adjectives to tell what kind.

The Ranch

Amy and Josh live in a city.
They visit a busy ranch.

Is the ranch crowded? Amy and Josh have room to ride strong horses.

The last day they feed a cow. They have a fun time!

Writing Trait Sentences
The writer uses different kinds of sentences.

Genre Realistic Story
Amy and Josh are like real children.

These **adjectives** tell what kind of ranch, what kind of horses, and what kind of time they have.

Conventions

● **Adjectives for What Kind**

An **adjective** can tell what kind.

● **Happy** children pick **ripe** berries.

Genre
Procedural Text

Read Together

● A sign gives us information. It may tell us what something is, where to go, what to do, or what to watch out for.

● A symbol is something that stands for something else.

● Picture symbols give a lot of information in a small space.

● Warning signs are usually yellow diamonds with black symbols. This makes them easy to spot.

● As you read "On the Way to a Ranch," look for signs and symbols and explain what they mean.

On the Way to a RANCH

We are going to a ranch. We will see signs and symbols along the way. They will help us.

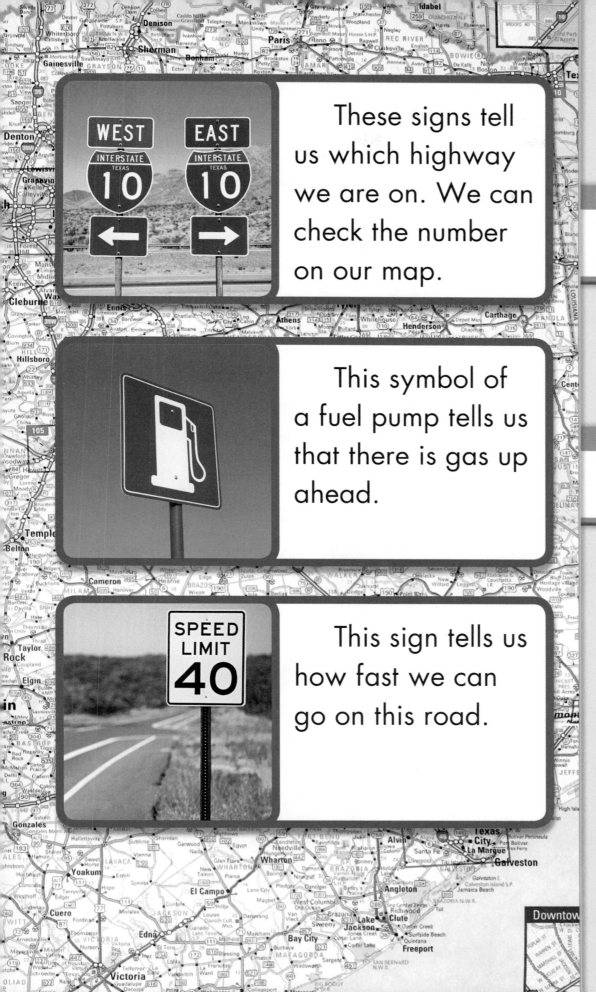

These signs tell us which highway we are on. We can check the number on our map.

This symbol of a fuel pump tells us that there is gas up ahead.

This sign tells us how fast we can go on this road.

Let's **Think** About...

What information is on these signs?
Procedural Text

Let's **Think** About...

Why do many signs use symbols?
Procedural Text

Signs that are yellow and diamond-shaped tell us to watch out.

Let's **Think** About...

Why are warning signs usually the same color and shape?
Procedural Text

This sign tells us to watch out for cattle.

This sign tells us to watch out for horse riders.

150

What does this sign mean?

This sign tells us we are there! We are at the ranch.

Let's **Think** About...

What does this sign and symbol mean?
Procedural Text

Let's **Think** About...

Retell the order of events in the text using the words.
Procedural Text

Let's **Think** About...

Reading Across Texts Which sign in "On the Way to a Ranch" do you think is most likely to be on or near the ranch in *A Southern Ranch*? Why?

Writing Across Texts Draw a sign that could be posted near a roundup, like the one in *A Southern Ranch*. Write about what the sign means and why you chose it.

Let's Learn It!

Media Literacy

Use television, newspapers, and the Internet to find information.

Purposes of Media Television, newspapers, and the Internet can give us information about the weather, people, sports, and other news.

Practice It! Watch a weather report on television or look at a weather map in a newspaper. Take notes. Share the information you learned with others. Use adjectives such as *cool, hot, sunny,* or *rainy.*

Vocabulary

Some words sound alike but mean different things. **Context clues** can help show the meaning of a word.

I **heard** the bells ringing.
The **herd** of cattle ate grass.

Heard and *herd* sound the same but have different spellings and different meanings.

Practice It! Read these words. Write a sentence with each word. Have a partner read your sentences and use context clues to tell the meanings of the words below.

read   red   plane   plain

Fluency

Accuracy, Rate, and Expression
When you read, try to read without making mistakes. Use your voice to show feeling.

Practice It!

1. Eight wrens flew high into the sky.

2. Will you laugh if I wear a bright hat?

Oral Vocabulary

Let's Talk About

Read Together

Treasures to Share

● Share ideas about what it means to share a treasure.

● Share information about treasures we can share at home.

READING STREET ONLINE
CONCEPT TALK VIDEO
www.ReadingStreet.com

Objectives
- Know how a word changes when one of its sounds is changed.
- Combine sounds together to say words with one and two syllables.
- Pick out sounds at the beginning, in the middle, and at the end of one-syllable words.

Phonemic Awareness

Let's Listen for

Read Together

Sounds

● Find five things that contain the long *u* sound.

● Find the animal in the new suit. Change the sound /n/ in *new* to the sound /t/. Say the new word.

● Find three things that are compound words.

● Find a word that rhymes with *suit*. Say the sound in the middle of the word.

READING STREET ONLINE
SOUND-SPELLING CARDS
www.ReadingStreet.com

156

157

Envision It! | Sounds to Know

football

compound word

**READING STREET ONLINE
SOUND-SPELLING CARDS**
www.ReadingStreet.com

Phonics

🔊 Compound Words

Words I Can Blend

p o p c o r n

p ea n u t s

d ay d r ea m

c l a s s m a t e

i n s i d e

Sentences I Can Read

1. Carmen thinks popcorn with peanuts is the best snack.

2. We can daydream while we rest at home.

3. Let's run inside and ask my classmate Luke.

Words I Can Read

stood

room

thought

picture

remember

Sentences I Can Read

1. Karl stood up tall to reach that flashlight in his room.

2. We thought he might play in that softball game.

3. Did he remember that picture of those catfish?

Envision It! | **Sounds to Know**

glue

ue

newt

ew

fruit

ui

160

Phonics

Vowel Digraphs
ue, ew, ui

Words I Can Blend

t	r	ue	
g	r	ew	
f	r	ui	t
g	l	ue	
n	ew		

Sentences I Can Read

1. Is it true that he grew?

2. We like eating fresh fruit.

3. She can glue that vase to make it like new.

This morning Sue stood in her room. She looked at her new bedspread. It was so nice! It had this picture of a rainbow by a seashore, with sailboats in back.

Sue thought about that trip her family made to the seaside last year. It was fun to remember when she kept her swimsuit on all day long and swam. Will her family go back next year?

You've learned

- Compound Words
- Vowel Digraphs *ue, ew, ui*

High-Frequency Words

stood   room   thought
picture   remember

PETER'S CHAIR

by Ezra Jack Keats

Realistic fiction has make-believe characters who act like real people. Next you will read about a boy who has a new baby sister.

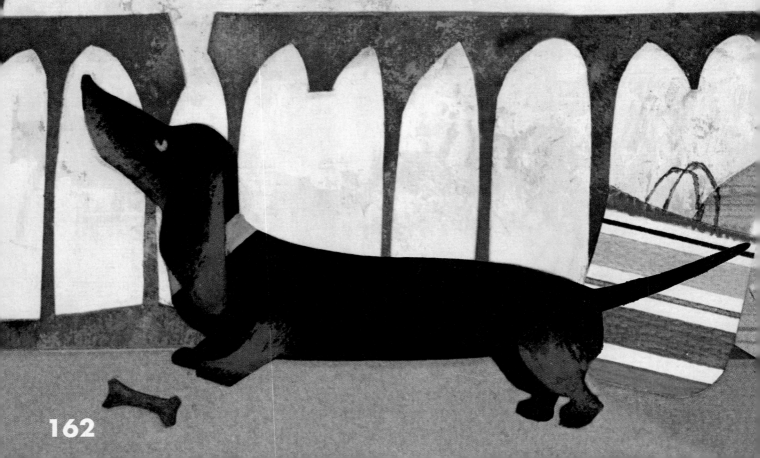

Question of the Week

What treasures can we share at home?

Peter stretched as high as he could.
There! His tall building was finished.

CRASH! Down it came.

"Shhhh!" called his mother. "You'll have to play more quietly. Remember, we have a new baby in the house."

Peter looked into his sister Susie's room.
His mother was fussing around the cradle.

"That's my cradle," he thought, "and they
painted it pink!"

"Hi, Peter," said his father. "Would
you like to help paint Sister's high chair?"
"It's my high chair," whispered Peter.

He saw his crib and muttered, "My crib. It's painted pink too."

Not far away stood his old chair.

"They didn't paint that yet!" Peter shouted.

He picked it up and ran to his room.

"Let's run away, Willie," he said. Peter filled
a shopping bag with cookies and dog biscuits.

"We'll take my blue chair, my toy crocodile, and the picture of me when I was a baby."
Willie got his bone.

They went outside and stood in
front of his house.

"This is a good place," said Peter.
He arranged his things very nicely and
decided to sit in his chair for a while.

But he couldn't fit in
the chair. He was too big!

His mother came to the window and called,
"Won't you come back to us, Peter dear? We
have something very special for lunch."

Peter and Willie made believe they didn't
hear. But Peter got an idea.

Soon his mother saw signs that Peter was home. "That rascal is hiding behind the curtain," she said happily.

She moved the curtain
away. But he wasn't there!

"Here I am," shouted Peter.

Peter sat in a grown-up chair.
His father sat next to him.

"Daddy," said Peter, "let's paint the little chair pink for Susie."

And they did.

Envision It! | Retell

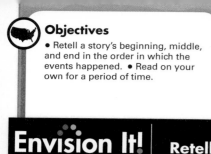

READING STREET ONLINE
STORY SORT
www.ReadingStreet.com

182

Think Critically

1. Did you understand why Peter was sad? Have you ever felt the way Peter did? Text to Self

2. Why do you think the author wrote this story? Author's Purpose

3. What does Peter learn in this story? Theme

4. How does Peter feel at the beginning of the story? How does he feel at the end?

   Story Structure

5. **Look Back and Write** Look back at pages 168–169. Why does Peter take his chair to his room? Write about it.

   TEST PRACTICE | Extended Response

Ezra Jack Keats

Ezra Jack Keats was an artist and author. He grew up in Brooklyn, New York, and often wrote about city life.

His first story about Peter, *The Snowy Day,* won the Caldecott Medal and made him famous. Mr. Keats died in 1983.

Here are more books by Ezra Jack Keats.

 Use the Reading Log in the *Reader's and Writer's Notebook* to record your independent reading.

Objectives
● Write short letters that put your ideas in an order that makes sense and uses the correct features.
● Understand and use adjectives when reading, writing, and speaking.

Let's Write It!

Read Together

Key Features of a Thank-You Note

● thanks someone for doing something nice

● tells how the writer feels

READING STREET ONLINE
GRAMMAR JAMMER
www.ReadingStreet.com

Expressive

Thank-You Note

A **thank-you note** tells a person who did something nice that you are thankful. The student model on the next page is an example of a thank-you note.

Writing Prompt Think about someone who shared something with you. Write a note to thank the person.

Writer's Checklist

Remember, you should . . .

☑ tell about why you are glad this person shared with you.

☑ use number words to show how many.

☑ write the date, a letter greeting, and a closing.

May 5, 2010

Dear Kim,

Thank you for sharing three books with me.

Now I have read them. My favorite book was the one about two dogs.

Your friend,
Tamara

Writing Trait Conventions Capital letters, punctuation, and correct spelling help readers understand your writing.

These **adjectives** tell how many.

Genre Thank-You Note This writer used words to say thanks.

Conventions

- **Adjectives for How Many**

  Some **adjectives** tell how many.

- Did Peter pack **many** crackers and **four** dog treats?

Objectives
• Understand the reasons for different types of media with help from a teacher or a parent.

21st Century Skills
INTERNET GUY

Read Together

E-mail is great! E-mail other students around the world. Work on a project together. Make our world a better place. Or, read a good book together. Then share your ideas by e-mail.

- Using a computer and the Internet, people can send messages across long distances very quickly. These messages are called e-mails.

- The purpose of an e-mail is to communicate quickly.

- E-mails are sent to people's e-mail addresses.

- Writing and sending e-mails is quick and easy. Type your message, and then click SEND.

Peter's Baby Sister

Peter lives far from his grandmother. They share news by e-mail. See how.
1. Peter types his e-mail.

| Write | Reply | Send | Forward | Delete | Address | Print |

Hi, Grandma!

I have a new little sister.
Did you have a little sister?
What was it like?
Please come to see us.

Peter

186

2. Then Peter clicks his mouse on the SEND button. In a flash, Grandma gets Peter's e-mail.

3. Grandma reads Peter's e-mail.

4. Then she writes back.

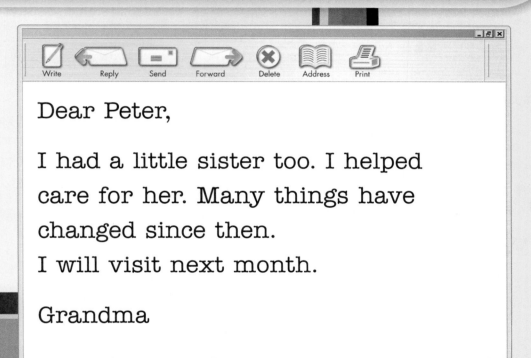

Write   Reply   Send   Forward   Delete   Address   Print

Dear Peter,

I had a little sister too. I helped care for her. Many things have changed since then.
I will visit next month.

Grandma

for more practice

Get Online!
www.ReadingStreet.com
Write an e-mail to a relative.

21st Century Skills Online Activity
Log on and follow the step-by-step online activity to write an e-mail.

Objectives
● Read fluently and understand texts at your grade level. ● Put a series of words in alphabetical order based on the first or second letters. Use a dictionary to find words.
● Understand the reasons for different types of media with help from a teacher or a parent.

Let's
Learn
It!

Read Together

Get Ready For Grade 2

When you watch a television program, recognize its purpose.

Media Literacy

Purposes of Media Books, films, television, and the Internet can be sources of both fun and information. We can read funny stories, watch movies about animal life cycles, and play fun games.

Practice It! Ask your teacher to help you use the Internet to find a Web site that you find interesting. Share what you find with others. Let others share what they find with you. Discuss whether what you found is informational or entertaining.

Vocabulary

Words in a **dictionary** or **glossary** are in alphabetical order. If two words start with the same letter, look at the second letter.

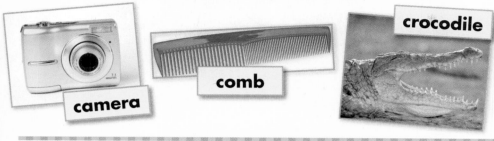

camera

comb

crocodile

These words are in alphabetical order.

Practice It! Read these words. Write them in alphabetical order. Then use a dictionary to find them.

straight   splash   shiny

Fluency

Appropriate Phrasing When you see a comma, pause for a moment as you read. It is important to pay attention to punctuation within a sentence as well as at the end.

Practice It!

1. After lunch, Sam stood next to the blue sandbox.

2. "Jen, take a picture of the campfire," said Brent.

3. He thought we had fruit, bread, and milk.

Objectives
● Listen closely to speakers and ask questions to help you better understand the topic. ● Share information and ideas about the topic. Speak at the correct pace.

Oral Vocabulary

Let's Talk About

Treasures to Share

● Share ideas about what it means to share a treasure.

● Share information about kinds of treasures we can share with neighbors.

Objectives

• Know how a word changes when one of its sounds is changed.
• Combine sounds together to say words with one and two syllables.
• Pick out sounds at the beginning, in the middle, and at the end of one-syllable words.

Let's Listen for

Sounds

Read Together

● Find five pictures that contain the vowel sound in *moon*.

● Find something that rhymes with *spoon*. Change the first sound in the word to the sound /s/. Say the new word.

● Find something that rhymes with *room*. Say the sound in the middle of that word. Now say the sound at the end of the word.

READING STREET ONLINE
SOUND-SPELLING CARDS
www.ReadingStreet.com

192

Objectives
● Identify and read at least 100 words from a list of words that you use often.
● Read words with common suffixes.

Envision It! | Sounds to Know

loudly

suffix -ly

cheerful

suffix -ful

READING STREET ONLINE
SOUND-SPELLING CARDS
www.ReadingStreet.com

Phonics

 # Suffixes *-ly, -ful*

Words I Can Blend

s l ow l y

s a d l y

th a n k f u l

p l ay f u l

u s e f u l

Sentences I Can Read

1. Billy walked home slowly and sadly when his team lost.

2. I am thankful for my playful kitten.

3. Tools can be useful for tasks.

Words I Can Read

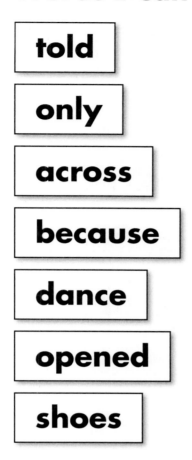

told

only

across

because

dance

opened

shoes

Sentences I Can Read

1. Suddenly the sky opened up and the rain fell across the fields.

2. I only dance in shoes that are not harmful to my feet.

3. Mom told me to dress quickly because we were late.

Envision It! | **Sounds to Know**

moon

oo

READING STREET ONLINE
SOUND-SPELLING CARDS
www.ReadingStreet.com

Phonics

Vowel Sound in *moon: oo*

Words I Can Blend

| b | r | oo | m |

| b | oo | t | s |

| s | p | oo | n |

| f | oo | d |

| t | oo |

Sentences I Can Read

1. Use that broom to sweep mud off those boots.

2. My little sister uses a spoon.

3. Is that food too hot?

I Can Read!

One cool day Jill's mom told her, "Walk quickly and safely across Green Field because dance class starts soon."

When Jill got to class, she opened her bag and grabbed her new shoes.

Jill had fun in class. "Oops!" she said when she made only one mistake.

Cheerful and helpful classmates showed her the right steps.

You've learned

- Suffixes -ly, -ful
- Vowel Sound in *moon*: oo

High-Frequency Words
told only across because
dance opened shoes

Henry and Mudge

and

Mrs. Hopper's House

by Cynthia Rylant

illustrated by Carolyn Bracken
in the style of Suçie Stevenson

Genre **Realistic fiction** has settings that seem real, but the stories are made up. Next you will find out what happens when Henry and Mudge visit a neighbor.

A Sweetheart Dance

Valentine's Day was coming. Henry and his big dog Mudge loved Valentine's Day because of the candy. They liked the candy hearts that said "You're swell" and "Oh, dear" and things like that.

Henry read the words, and Mudge licked
them off. They were a good team.

On this Valentine's Day Henry's father and Henry's mother were going to a Sweetheart Dance. Henry and Mudge would be staying with Mrs. Hopper.

Mrs. Hopper lived across the street in a big stone house with droopy trees and dark windows and a gargoyle on the door.

Henry liked Mrs. Hopper. But he did not like her house.

"Are you sure Mudge and I can't come to the Sweetheart Dance?" Henry asked his father.

"Only if you both promise to wear a tuxedo and shiny black shoes and waltz to 'The Blue Danube,'" said Henry's father.

Henry looked at Mudge and tried to imagine him in a tuxedo and shiny black shoes, waltzing to "The Blue Danube."

"I think we'd better go to Mrs. Hopper's," Henry said.

"Good idea," said Henry's father.

"Because Mudge only knows how to tap-dance," Henry said with a grin.

Costumes

Mrs. Hopper wasn't like anyone Henry had ever met. She played the violin for him. She served him tea. She told him about her father, who had been a famous actor.

She was very kind to Mudge. She cooked him a bowl of oatmeal and gave him his own loaf of French bread.

After the tea and music and oatmeal,
Mrs. Hopper took them upstairs. She opened
a room that had been her father's.

"Wow!" said Henry. The room was full
of costumes.

There were silk capes and tall hats and shiny coats. There were canes and swords and umbrellas. There were wigs.

Mrs. Hopper put a wig on Mudge.
"You look like a poodle, Mudge!"
said Henry.
Mudge wagged and wagged.

Henry and Mudge and Mrs. Hopper spent most of the evening in the costume room. They had a wonderful time.

And when Henry's parents came back from the dance, were they ever surprised. Mudge was a poodle, and Henry was a man! Henry wore a tuxedo and a hat and shiny black shoes.

"I bet you didn't know I was this handsome," Henry told his dad. And everyone laughed and laughed.

Objectives
• Tell what you think will happen. Read the part that tells what happens.
• Retell a story's beginning, middle, and end in the order in which the events happened. • Read on your own for a period of time.

Envision It! | Retell

READING STREET ONLINE
STORY SORT
www.ReadingStreet.com

Think Critically

1. Which would you rather do on Valentine's Day—what Henry did or what his parents did? Tell why you think as you do. Text to Self

2. Why do you think the author wrote this story? Author's Purpose

3. Why did Mrs. Hopper have so many costumes?

Cause and Effect

4. Look back at page 213. Read the part that tells what was in Mrs. Hopper's room. Did you predict correctly?

Predict and Set Purpose

5. Look Back and Write Look back at pages 214–216. What costumes do Henry and Mudge try on? Write about them.

TEST PRACTICE | Extended Response

Cynthia Rylant

Cynthia Rylant grew up in West Virginia. She says, "I lived in a place called Cool Ridge, in a four-room house with my grandparents. We had no running water, and my grandparents grew and hunted most of our food."

Ms. Rylant has written many books about Henry and Mudge. Now she lives in Oregon with her dogs Martha Jane and Gracie Rose.

Here are more Henry and Mudge books.

Reading Log

Use the Reading Log in the *Reader's and Writer's Notebook* to record your independent reading.

Let's Write It!

Key Features of Directions

● give details about how to do something

● should be clear and easy to understand

READING STREET ONLINE
GRAMMAR JAMMER
www.ReadingStreet.com

Expository

Directions

Directions tell how to complete a task. The student model on the next page is an example of directions.

Writing Prompt Think about how people make surprise gifts and plan fun activities for others. Write directions telling how to make a gift or plan a fun activity to surprise someone.

Writer's Checklist

Remember, you should . . .

☑ tell all the steps.

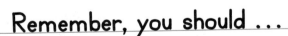
☑ put the steps in the right order.

☑ use adjectives that compare.

How to Plan a Game

First find out about a game your friend likes.

Next, ask your friend to come over.

Then play the game with your friend.

Your friend will have the biggest smile ever!

Writing Trait Organization These steps are in the proper order.

Genre Directions These **directions** are easy to understand.

Biggest is an **adjective** that compares one smile to all other smiles.

Conventions

Adjectives That Compare

Remember Add **-er** to an adjective to compare two persons, places, animals, or things. Add **-est** to an adjective to compare more than two persons, places, animals, or things.

Genre
Poetry

- A poem often expresses the poet's feelings about something. A poem is written in lines and stanzas.

- Often a poem has rhyming words at the ends of some lines. A poem may also have alliteration, or words with the same beginning sounds.

- A poem usually has rhythm, or a regular pattern of beats.

- Think about what you know about rhyme, rhythm, and alliteration as you read these poems.

Good Books, Good Times!

by Lee Bennett Hopkins
illustrated by Luciana Navarro Alves

Good books.

Good times.

Good stories.

Good rhymes.

Good beginnings.

Good ends.

Good people.

Good friends.

Good fiction.

Good facts.

Good adventures.

Good acts.

Good stories.

Good rhymes.

Good books.

Good times.

Dress-Up

by Bobbi Katz
illustrated by Luciana Navarro Alves

A treasure chest of castoff clothes!
What's more fun, do you suppose?
With dandy costumes such as these
we can dress up as we please!
A tie, a hat, a string of beads—
are just the things
that each kid needs!
Be a hunter or an elf—
be *anyone* . . . except yourself!

Let's **Think** About...

Which words **rhyme** in the poems on these pages?

Shell

by Myra Cohn Livingston
illustrated by Luciana Navarro Alves

When it was time
for Show and Tell,
Adam brought a big pink shell.

He told about
the ocean roar
and walking on the
sandy shore.

And then he passed
the shell around.
We listened to the water sound.

And that's the first time
I could hear
the wild waves calling
to my ear.

Let's Think About...

What **sensory details** can you find? What do they help you see and hear?

Let's Think About...

What is the **alliteration** in the last stanza of this poem?

Reading

by Marchette Chute
illustrated by Luciana Navarro Alves

A story is a special thing.
    The ones that I have read,
They do not stay inside the book,
    They stay inside my head.

The Rainbow

by Iain Crichton Smith
illustrated by Luciana Navarro Alves

The rainbow's like a colored bridge
that sometimes shines from
    ridge to ridge.
Today one end is in the sea,
the other's in the field with me.

Let's Think About...

What is the **rhythm** in each poem? Clap the beats as you read them.

Let's Think About...

Reading Across Texts In *Henry and Mudge and Mrs. Hopper's House,* Henry and Mrs. Hopper share treasures. The poems share treasures with readers. Describe all of these treasures.

Writing Across Texts Write a short poem about something you treasure. Tell how you could share it with someone else. Use rhythm, rhyme, and alliteration in your poem.

225

Let's **Learn** It!

Read Together

READING STREET ONLINE
VOCABULARY ACTIVITIES
www.ReadingStreet.com

Get Ready For Grade 2

As you watch television, decide if you are being entertained or informed.

Media Literacy

Purposes of Media When the media gives us news or facts about a topic, we are being informed. When the media tells us stories or makes us laugh, we are being entertained.

Practice It! Think of something you saw on television, on the Internet, or in a newspaper. Did it inform you or entertain you? Tell how. Use adjectives as you describe what you saw.

Vocabulary

A **compound word** is a word made from two smaller words. To find the meaning of the compound word, look at the meanings of the two short words.

> A *fish* is an animal that lives in water. A *bowl* is a container that holds water or food. A *fishbowl* is a compound word that means "a bowl where a fish lives."

Practice It! Read these words. Tell the meaning of each smaller word, and then tell the meaning of the compound word.

lunchtime   **grasshopper**

Fluency

Expression and Intonation When you read, try to read the sentences as if you were talking. Use your voice to show feeling.

Practice It!

1. Kate told us to swim quickly.

2. I love the dance shoes Dad bought me!

biscuits • castle

Bb

biscuits **Biscuits** are small cakes of bread that are not sweet.

break To **break** something means to make it come apart into pieces. If I drop a plate, it might **break**.

buñuelos **Buñuelos** are sweet pastries that are fried and then covered with sugar. **Buñuelos** are like doughnuts, but smaller.

Cc

capital The **capital** of a country is the city where the government is located. The **capital** of the United States is Washington, D.C.

castle

castle A **castle** is a large stone building with thick walls and a tower. Long ago, kings and queens lived in **castles**.

cattle **Cattle** are animals raised for their meat, milk, or skins. Cows and bulls are **cattle.**

cattle

coach A **coach** is a large, usually closed carriage with seats inside and often on top. Long ago, most **coaches** were pulled by a team of horses.

confetti • country

confetti Confetti is bits of colored paper thrown during celebrations. We threw confetti at the birthday party.

confetti

cookies Cookies are small, flat, sweet cakes.

country A country is a land of a group of people who have the same government. The United States is a country in North America.

cow A **cow** is a large farm animal that gives milk.

cradle A **cradle** is a small bed for a baby, usually one that can rock from side to side.

crocodile A **crocodile** is a large reptile with thick skin, four short legs, and a pointed nose. **Crocodiles** look a lot like alligators.

crocodile

curtain A **curtain** is a cloth or other material hung across a window. **Curtains** are often used to keep out light.

document • gargoyle

Dd

document A **document** is something written or printed that gives information. Letters, maps, and pictures are **documents.**

Ff

front The **front** of something is the first part or beginning of it. If you are in **front,** you are ahead of the rest.

Gg

gargoyle A **gargoyle** is a decoration. It usually is made of stone and shaped like a scary animal or person. **Gargoyles** often decorate buildings.

gargoyle

government A **government** is a group of people who manage a country. Our **government** includes the President, the Congress, and the Supreme Court.

guitar A **guitar** is a musical instrument that usually has six strings. You play a **guitar** with your fingers.

guitar

happily • married

Hh

happily If you do something
happily, you do it in a happy way.
They lived **happily** ever after.

heart A **heart** is a figure
shaped like this.
The card was covered with **hearts**.

heart

Ii

idea An **idea** is a thought or plan.
It was my **idea** to go to the zoo.

Mm

married If two people get **married,**
they become husband and wife.

Pp

piñata

piñata A **piñata** is a decorated pottery pot filled with candy, fruit, and small toys. Blindfolded children swing sticks in order to break the **piñata** and get what is inside.

point In cattle herding, ranch hands on horseback who "ride **point**" ride in front of the herd.

prince A **prince** is a son of a king or queen.

present A **present** is a gift. A **present** is something that someone gives you or that you give someone. His uncle sent him a birthday **present.**

present

pumpkin • tortilla

pumpkin A **pumpkin** is a large orange fruit that grows on a vine.

pumpkin

Rr

roundup A **roundup** is a gathering together of cattle or other large animals.

Ss

shiny Something that is **shiny** is bright. Mom gave me a **shiny** new penny.

sold If something is **sold,** it is given to someone in exchange for money.

Tt

tortilla A **tortilla** is a thin, flat, round bread made of cornmeal. **Tortillas** are baked on a flat surface and can be filled with rice, meat, beans, and other foods.

tuxedo A **tuxedo** is a formal suit for boys and men. **Tuxedos** are usually black.

tuxedo

twelve o'clock When it is **twelve o'clock,** it is either midday or midnight. **Twelve o'clock** can also be written as **12:00.**

Valentine's Day • waltz

Vv **Valentine's Day** **Valentine's Day** is February 14, a day when people send cards with hearts and small presents.

Ww **waltz** To **waltz** means to dance slowly with graceful steps. Mom and Dad like to **waltz** together.

waltz

woman A **woman** is a grown-up female person.

woman

wonderful If something is **wonderful**, you like it very much. The ocean was a **wonderful** sight. She had a **wonderful** time at the party.

Mama's Birthday Present

about
enjoy
give
surprise
worry
would

A Trip to Washington, D.C.

found
mouth
once
took
wild

Cinderella

colors
draw
drew
great
over
show
sign

A Southern Ranch

above
eight
laugh
moon
touch

Henry and Mudge and Mrs. Hopper's House

across
because
dance
only
opened
shoes
told

Peter's Chair

picture
remember
room
stood
thought

Aa Bb Cc

Dd Ee Ff

Gg Hh Ii

Jj Kk Ll

Mm Nn Oo

Pp Qq Rr

Ss Tt Uu

Vv Ww Xx

Yy Zz

Acknowledgments

Text

Grateful acknowledgment is made to the following for copyrighted material:

Carcanet Press Limited

"Rainbow" by Iain Crichton Smith from *A Scottish Poetry Book*. Copyright © 1983 Oxford University Press. Used by permission of Carcanet Press Limited.

Carmen Tafolla

"Mama's Birthday Present" by Carmen Tafolla. Used by permission of Carmen Tafolla.

Curtis Brown, Ltd.

"Good Books, Good Times" by Lee Bennett Hopkins. Copyright © 1995 by Lee Bennett Hopkins. First appeared in Good Rhymes, Good Times, published by HarperCollins. Used by permission of Curtis Brown, Ltd.

Elizabeth Hauser

"Reading" from *Rhymes About Us* by Marchette Chute, published 1974 by E.P. Dutton. Used by permission of Elizabeth Hauser.

Ezra Jack Keats Foundation

''Peter's Chair'' From *Peter's Chair* by Ezra Jack Keats. Copyright © 1967. Used by permission of Ezra Jack Keats Foundation.

Marian Reiner

"Shell" from *Worlds I Know and Other Poems* by Myra Cohn Livingston. Copyright © 1985 by Myra Cohn Livingston. Used by permission of Marian Reiner.

Random House Children's Books, a division of Random House, Inc.

"Dress Up" by Bobbi Katz from *Poems for Small Friends* by Bobbi Katz. Copyright © 1989 by Random House, Inc. Illustrations © 1989 by Gyo Fujikawa. Used by permission of Random House Children's Books, a division of Random House, Inc. For on-line information about other Random House, Inc. books and authors, see the Internet website at http://www.randomhouse.com.

Simon & Schuster Books for Young Readers, an imprint of Simon & Schuster Children's Publishing Division

Reprinted with the permission of Simon Spotlight, an imprint of Simon & Schuster Children's Publishing Division from *Henry And Mudge And Mrs. Hopper's House* by Cynthia Rylant. Text copyright © 2003 by Cynthia Rylant.

Note: Every effort has been made to locate the copyright owner of material reproduced on this component. Omissions brought to our attention will be corrected in subsequent editions.

Illustrations

Cover Daniel Moreton

14 John Ashton Golden

20 - 46 Gabriel Pacheco

54 George Ulrich

60 - 77 Paule Trudel Bellemare

82 - 85, 222 Luciana Navarro Powell

90 Guy Francis

96 - 109 Dean MacAdam

122 Gabriel Carranza

158 Matt Luxich

196 Scott R. Brooks

PI7 Mary Anne Lloyd

Photographs

Every effort has been made to secure permission and provide appropriate credit for photographic material. The publisher deeply regrets any omission and pledges to correct errors called to its attention in subsequent editions.

Unless otherwise acknowledged, all photographs are the property of Pearson Education, Inc.

Photo locators denoted as follows: Top (T), Center (C), Bottom (B), Left (L), Right (R), Background (Bkgd)

10 ©Dianna Sarto/Corbis

12 ©Royalty-Free/Corbis

50 Purestock/Getty Images

52 ©Design Pics Inc./Alamy

98 ©David R. Frazier Phctolibrary, Inc./Alamy Images

100 Medioimages/Jupiter Images

102 Glowimages/Getty Images

103 (CR, CL) National Archives

104 ©Private Collection, Peter Newark American Pictures/Bridgeman Art Library

105 Getty Images

106 (TL) ©Jeff Vanuga/Corbis, (Bkgd) ©Skip Brown/National Geographic Image Collection

107 Corbis/Jupiter Images

108 Jupiter Images

109 ©Visions of America, LLC/Alamy

114 Creatas

115 (T) ©Ariel Skelley/Corbis, (B) ©Paul Barton/Corbis

116 Wayne Eastep/Getty Images

118 Getty Images

119 David Madison/Getty Images, Martin Barraud/Getty Images

120 ©David R. Frazier Photolibrary, Inc./Alamy Images, Jupiter Images

121 ©Steve Hamblin/Alamy

128 ©Christina Handley/Masterfile Corporation

130 ©Terry Husebye /Jupiter Images

131 ©Ron Chapple Stock/Corbis

132 (B) ©David Stoecklein/Corbis, (T) ©Ron Chapple Stock/Corbis

134 ©John Foster/Masterfile Corporation

136 Art Life Images

137 ©Carson Ganci/Design Pics/Corbis

138 ©Macduff Everton/Corbis

140 Buddy Mays/Corbis

142 ©Roy Ooms/Masterfile Corporation

143 Jupiter Images

148 ©Andersen Ross/Getty Images

149 (TR) ©Free Agents Limited/Corbis, (CR) ©Image Farm Inc./Alamy, (BR) ©Image Source/Getty Images

150 (TL) ©Jason Hosking /zefa//Corbis, (CL) ©L. Clarke/Corbis, (B) ©Witold Skrypczak/Alamy Images

152 ©Jupiter Images/Alamy

154 ©Don Mason/Corbis

188 Randy Faris/Corbis

189 ©Stockbyte, Digital Stock

190 Brooklyn Productions/Getty Images

227 81A Productions/Corbis

228 Getty Images

229 ©ImageState/Alamy Images

230 Corbis/Jupiter Images

239 Getty Images

244 ©Ianni Dimitrov/Alamy Images

245 Jupiter Images.

High-Frequency Words

Identify and read the high-frequency words that you have learned. How many words can you read?

Unit R.1
a
green
I
see

Unit R.2
like
one
we

Unit R.3
do
look
was
yellow
you

Unit R.4
are
have
that
they
two

Unit R.5
he
is
three
to
with

Unit R.6
for
go
here
me
where

Unit 1.1
come
my
way

Unit 1.2
she
take
up
what

Unit 1.3
blue
from
help
little
use

Unit 1.4
eat
five
four
her

this
too

Unit 1.5
saw
small
tree
your

Unit 1.6
home
into
many
them

Unit 2.1
catch
good
no
put
said
want

Unit 2.2
be
could
horse
of
old
paper

Unit 2.3
live
out
people
who
work

Unit 2.4
down
inside
now
there
together

Unit 2.5
around
find
food
grow
under
water

Unit 2.6
also
family
new
other
some
their

High-Frequency Words

Unit 3.1
always
become
day
everything
nothing
stays
things

Unit 3.2
any
enough
ever
every
own
sure
were

Unit 3.3
away
car
friends
house
our
school
very

Unit 3.4
afraid
again
few
how
read
soon

Unit 3.5
done
know
push
visit
wait

Unit 3.6
before
does
good-bye
oh
right
won't

Unit 4.1
about
enjoy
gives
surprise
worry
would

Unit 4.2
colors
draw
drew
great
over
show
sign

Unit 4.3
found

mouth
once
took
wild

Unit 4.4
above
eight
laugh
moon
touch

Unit 4.5
picture
remember
room
stood
thought

Unit 4.6
across
because
dance
only
opened
shoes
told

Unit 5.1
along
behind
eyes
never
pulling

toward

Unit 5.2
door
loved
should
wood

Unit 5.3
among
another
instead
none

Unit 5.4
against
goes
heavy
kinds
today

Unit 5.5
built
early
learn
science
through

Unit 5.6
answered
carry
different
poor